Spoonfuls of Time

Erika Bodden

Spoonfuls of Time © 2023 Erika Bodden

All rights reserved.

No part of this publication may be reproduced, stored in a retrieval system, or transmitted, in any form or by any means, electronic, mechanical, photocopying, recording or otherwise, without the prior written permission of the presenters.

Erika Bodden asserts the moral right to be identified as author of this work.

Presentation by *BookLeaf Publishing*

Web: www.bookleafpub.com

E-mail: info@bookleafpub.com

ISBN: 9789358316605

First edition 2023

I dedicate this book to my students: past, present, and future. Pursue your dreams with confidence; time will take care of itself.

ACKNOWLEDGEMENT

A heartfelt thank you to my parents, Marlene D. Bodden and Donald Bertly Bodden Jr., for introducing me to the power within written words.

PREFACE

A haiku poem does not rhyme and consists of three lines totaling seventeen syllables: five syllables in line one, seven syllables in line two, and five syllables in line three.

Sunset

At the horizon,
the sun sinks into the sea.
My soul is at peace.

The Ladybug

It halts its flutter
To land on me on purpose
And give me good luck.

Lost

Foreign surroundings,
Time— my only companion,
Cloaked pathways summon.

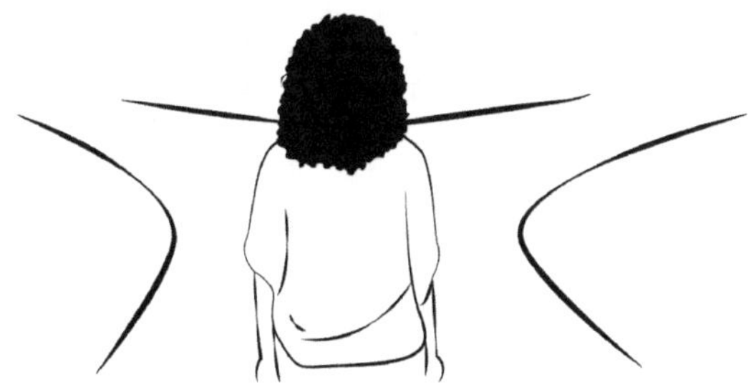

Contemplating

Copious options,
Meditative state of mind,
Decisions emerge.

Deep Breath

Catapulted start,
Adventurous leap of faith,
Bold dive into life.

Seasonal Shifts

Altered excursion,
Junctures illuminated,
En route to success.

Full Moon

Infinite beacon,
Indestructible promise,
Enormous comfort.

Birds

Delicate beauty,
Hovering in revelry,
Wonderment of grace.

Rest

Much needed respite,
Subliminal song relayed,
Spirit uplifted.

Dark Morning

Optimism smudged,
Aversions shrewdly exposed,
Stamina strengthened.

Bare Branches

Ornate labyrinth,
Intriguing ruminations,
Mysteries unfold.

Hibernation

Soft quilt of darkness,
Devoted slumber stands guard,
Time's weary eyes close.

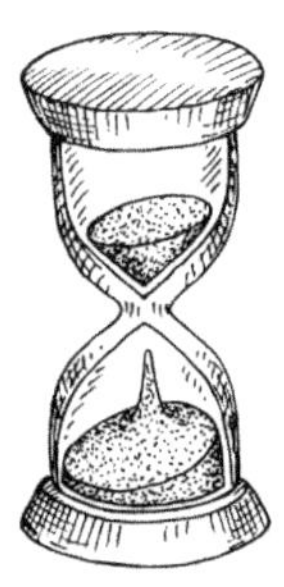

Cold Air

Bright morning sun yawns,
Sleepy sky stretches its arms,
Wintry wind waves hi.

Family

Affectionate warmth,
Sentimental anecdotes,
Everlasting bond.

By the Fire

Flames play hide and seek,
Smitten hearts chitter-chatter,
Sugary spell sings.

A Hot Drink

Serene ambience,
Flickering flames, chilly air,
Mug of cozy warmth.

Work of Art

With paintbrush in hand,
And the sun as a palette,
Winter paints the snow.

Winter Walk

Brisk air whistles tunes,
Excited clouds do cartwheels,
Vibrant sky applauds.

Winter Light

Dreams— born at midnight,
Swaddled tightly in moonbeams,
Cradled in shadows.

Leaving Behind

Dodging obstacles,
Shaking off uncertainties,
Soaring to great heights.

Hopeful

Wishes blazing bright,
My soul prepares for impact,
Imprints of zeal form.

www.ingramcontent.com/pod-product-compliance
Lightning Source LLC
LaVergne TN
LVHW050505210726
843509LV00015BA/3001